Elephants: 56 Fascinating Facts For Kids

Steve Robertson

This book is just one of a series of "Fascinating Facts For Kids" books. For more fascinating facts about people, history, animals and more please visit:

www.fascinatingfactsforkids.com

Contents

The Elephant's Ancestors

1. The ancestors of today's elephants were first seen more than 50 million years ago on the plains of Northern Africa.

2. The early elephant-like creatures were eventually found in all parts of the world except Antarctica and Australia. They lived in all types of habitat, including deserts, glaciers and rain forests.

3. There have been at least 26 species of elephants over the last 50 million years. Nowadays there are just 3 species, which live in the warm climates of Africa or Southern Asia.

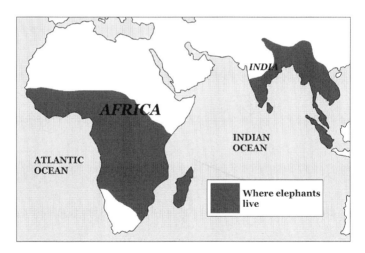

4. The most well known of the elephant's ancestors is the woolly mammoth, which roamed the frozen north during the Ice Age. Woolly

mammoths were covered in thick fur to help keep out the bitter cold.

5. Early humans hunted the woolly mammoth for food and also made tools from its tusks and bones, and clothing from its fur.

A woolly mammoth

6. The woolly mammoth became extinct around 10,000 years ago, when the last Ice Age ended and the climate became warmer.

7. The bodies of many mammoths were preserved in ice and because of this scientists have been able to find out more about the woolly mammoth than any other prehistoric animal.

8.   Not all the woolly mammoths died out following the Ice Age. A small number survived on Wrangel Island, which is off the north east coast of Russia, until around 4,000 years ago.

Types of Elephant

9. There are three types of elephant living today - the Asian, African bush and African forest elephants.

10. Asian elephants are found in the grasslands and forests of India and South East Asia. They have smaller tusks and ears than African elephants.

An Asian Elephant

11. The African bush elephant lives in the hot, open grasslands of Eastern and Southern Africa. They have long, curved tusks and massive ears.

An African bush elephant

12. The African forest elephant is found in the rain forests of Western and Central Africa. They are smaller than the African bush elephant and have darker skin.

An African forest elephant

The Trunk

13. The trunk is the elephant's nose, but as well as being used for smelling and breathing, it can do so much more.

14. An elephant can pick up objects as small as a seed or a flower using tips on the end of the trunk. African elephants have two tips and the Asian elephant just one.

15. An elephant uses its trunk to reach high into the trees to pull down fruit and leaves that other animals can't reach.

Reaching for food

16. An elephant uses the trunk for drinking. It sucks water into the trunk and when it is full the elephant lifts its head back before squirting the water from the trunk into the mouth.

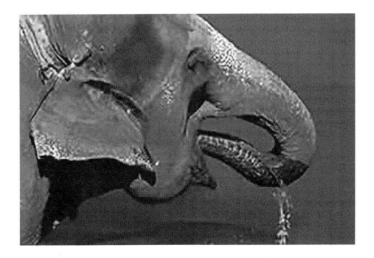

An elephant drinking

17. The trunk is very flexible, being made up of thousands of muscles and containing no bones. This means an elephant can stretch and move its trunk in all directions.

18. The trunk can be used to wipe an elephant's eyes, blow air onto the skin and spray water.

19. The trunk is so important that an elephant would find it impossible to survive if it was badly damaged.

Tusks & Teeth

20. The long, curved tusks of an elephant are in fact its two front teeth. Unlike the rest of the teeth, which are used for chewing and grinding food, the tusks are used as both tools and weapons.

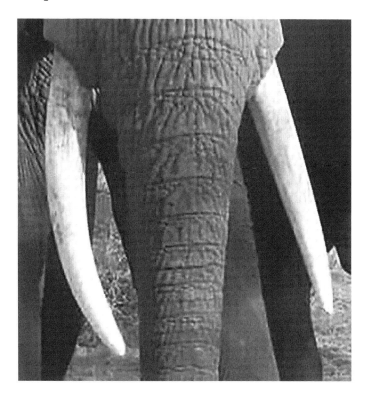

An elephant's tusks

21. Elephants use their tusks to dig in the soil when looking for roots to eat. Male elephants use their tusks for fighting and if the trunk gets tired it can be draped over the tusks to rest!

22. The tusks continue to grow throughout an elephant's life at around six inches (15 cm) a year. The tusks of an African male elephant can reach nearly 11½ feet (3.5 metres) in length.

23. As well as the tusks, elephants have 24 other teeth which are replaced six times during the animal's lifetime. They grow new sets of teeth so often because of all the chewing they have to do.

24. When an elephant reaches around 40 years of age it grows its last and largest set of teeth. Each tooth is around eight inches (21 cm) long and weighs nearly nine pounds (four kilograms).

Family Life

25. Elephants live together in family groups called 'herds'. The herd is led by an old female elephant, called the 'matriarch', which could be up to 70 years old.

26. The matriarch uses her age and experience to look after the other members of the herd, leading them to food and water.

27. A herd might contain 10-20 elephants, which will be all adult females, or 'cows', and their offspring. Adult male elephants live on their own or with other male adults.

A herd of elephants

28. When she reaches about 17 years old, a female elephant is old enough to produce babies, which are called 'calves'. A cow may have six or seven calves during her lifetime.

29. The adult females in a herd often produce their calves at the same time of year. These newborn baby elephants are looked after by all the female members of the herd.

A cow and its calf

30. As the herd gets larger with the arrival of more and more young elephants, some of the females and their calves may leave to form their own herd.

31. Young male elephants, or 'bulls', will stay with their mothers for around 10 years, when they are thrown out of the herd by the females. They will then live on their own or join small groups of other bulls.

32. Male elephants are ready to mate when they reach 25 years of age. Bulls will then fight with each other and the winner will get to mate with a female.

33. Bull elephants use their trunks and tusks to fight with. They are not often badly injured though, as an elephant will back down when it knows it has lost a fight.

Bull elephants fighting

34. When a male and female elephant produce their calf the bull will show little interest in its new offspring. He will leave to go back to its male way of life, leaving the female herd members to bring up his baby.

Food & Drink

35. Elephants are herbivores, or plant eaters. They eat grass, tree branches, leaves, tree bark, fruit, flowers and seeds.

36. Elephants spend up to 18 hours a day feeding. An adult elephant can get through 440 pounds (200 kg) of food every day.

37. Elephants use their long trunks to reach fruit and leaves high up in the trees or to pull grass from the ground. Their tusks and toes are used to dig for roots in the soil.

38. The bark from trees is one of the most nutritious foods an elephant can eat. Using its tusks to tear off the bark, it can take hours to completely strip a tree. With all the bark removed, the tree may not survive for long.

Stripping the bark off a tree

39. Elephants need around 18 gallons (70 litres) of water every day, but they can get through a lot more. An adult male can drink 55 gallons in under five minutes - enough to fill 40 buckets!

Keeping Cool

40. Elephants live in hot parts of the world so they often need to cool down. If they are near a waterhole or a river they can splash in the water or go for a swim. They also cover themselves in mud or dust to help keep cool.

Keeping cool in the mud

41. African bush elephants have the largest ears of any animal in the world and they help to keep their bodies cool. When an elephant flaps its ears the breeze created cools down the blood inside them. This blood then travels to other parts of the body to keep the elephant's temperature down.

42. An elephant can give itself a cooling shower by filling its trunk before swinging it and squirting water to every part of its body.

43. Elephants have wrinkly skin and all these wrinkles trap water when they have a shower. These means that the water takes a long time to evaporate and keeps the elephant cooler than if it had a smooth skin.

44. African forest elephants have much smaller ears than the bush elephant. It is thought the reason for this is that because they live in the cooler, shady forest they do not need such big ears to keep cool.

Communication & Intelligence

45. Elephants can produce a variety of sounds which they use to communicate with each other. They also use touch and body language.

46. When it is excited, scared or angry an elephant makes a loud trumpeting sound by blowing air out of its trunk. The sound can be heard up to six miles (10 kilometres) away.

47. Elephants can make a deep rumbling sound, too low for the human ear to hear. The vibrations produced by this sound can travel through the ground for up to 5½ miles (9 kilometres). Other elephants can detect these vibrations with their feet!

48. When a group of elephants are huddled together they may be talking to each other by using the rumbling sound, or perhaps to other elephants miles away.

49. When elephants meet each other they say hello by entwining their trunks, sniffing each other and rumbling a greeting.

Saying hello

50. Elephants are intelligent animals with large brains. Those that live close to humans learn to do the things we do, such as opening doors and turning on taps. Elephants in zoos have even painted pictures using a paintbrush held with their trunks!

Assorted Elephant Facts

51. A male African bull elephant can measure up to 30 feet (9 metres) from the end of its trunk to the tip of its tail.

52. Elephants are very good swimmers, capable of swimming distances of several miles. They can even swim underwater and breathe by using their trunks as snorkels.

53. Elephants can walk for up to 50 miles (80 kilometres) a day. They have soft, spongy cushions on the bottom of their feet, which means they walk almost silently.

54. Asian elephants are gentle creatures and for centuries they have been tamed by humans. They have been used to help with farming, carrying heavy loads and even in warfare.

55. Hannibal, a general from Carthage in North Africa, fought against the Romans over 2,000 years ago. He led an army of 50,000 men and 40 elephants across the Alps towards Rome. The horses of the Roman army were frightened by the elephants and Hannibal won three battles. But even with his elephants he couldn't conquer the mighty Roman army.

56. Elephants have been worshipped as gods in some cultures for centuries. The best known is the Hindu god of wisdom, Ganesh, who has the head of an elephant. Statues of elephants can be found at temples in many parts of Asia.

Ganesh, the Hindu god of wisdom

For more in the Fascinating Facts For Kids series, please visit:

www.fascinatingfactsforkids.com

Illustration Attributions

An Asian elephant   Khan-Tanvir

**An African forest
elephant**   Thomas Breuer

Reaching for food   Charlesjsharp

**An elephant
drinking**   Barbara Piuma

**Stripping the bark
off a tree**   Yathin S Krishnappa

Saying hello   jinterwas

56705916R00018

Made in the USA
San Bernardino, CA
13 November 2017